INDIA
In the Past and Present

Susan E. Goodman

PICTURE CREDITS
Cover © Anthony Cassidy/Getty Images; title page © Andrea Pistolesi/Getty Images; pages 2–3, 12 (bottom right), 32 © Jeremy Horner/Corbis; page 4 map illustrations by Paul Mirocha; page 5 (top left) © David Samuel Robbins/Corbis; page 5 (top right) © Peter Adams/Getty Images; pages 5, 6–7, 30 (bottom left), 31 (bottom left) © Ric Ergenbright/Corbis; page 5 (bottom right) © Dinodia Photo Library/Getty Images; pages 6–13 (borders) © Cathy Melloan; page 8 (top) © Borromeo/Art Resource, NY; page 8 (bottom), 34-c, 35-b © Lindsay Hebberd/Corbis; pages 9, 18, 34-b © Chris Lisle/Corbis; page 10 © Hugh Sitton/Getty Images; pages 11, 34-e © Patrick Ward/Corbis; pages 12 (top left), 29, 31 (center left) © Neil Emmerson/Getty Images; page 12 (top right) © Howard Davies/Corbis; page 12 (bottom left) © Bruno Morandi/Getty Images; pages 13, 25 (top left), 34-a © David Beatty/Getty Images; page 14 (top) © National Museum of India, New Delhi, India, Giraudon/Bridgeman Art Library; pages 14 (bottom), 30 (top left), 35-a, © British Library, London, UK/Bridgeman Art Library; pages 15, 25 (top right), 30 (top right) © HIP/Art Resource, NY; pages 16–17, 31 (center right) © Carl & Ann Purcell/Corbis; pages 19, 31 (top right) © Tiziana and Gianni Baldizzone/Corbis; pages 20, 25 (bottom left), 31 (top left) © Amit Gupta/Reuters/Corbis; page 21 © Earl & Nazima Kowall/Corbis; pages 22, 30 (bottom right) © Gavriel Jecan/Corbis; pages 23, 25 (bottom right), 31 (bottom right) © John Henry Claude Wilson/Getty Images; page 26 © Martin Puddy/Getty Images; pages 27, 34-d © Suzanne & Nick Geary/Getty Images; page 28 © Michael Freeman/Corbis; page 33 (left) India: Civilizations Past to Present by Ann M. Rossi © 2004 National Geographic Society, photo © Michael Freeman/Corbis; page 33 (center) West Asia: People and Places by Eden Force Eskin © 2003 National Geographic Society, photos (left) © Marilyn Gibbons/NGIC, (top right) © Michael Yamashita, (center right) © James P. Blair/NGIC, (bottom right) James Stanfield/NGIC; page 33 (right) West Asia: Geography and Environments by Robert Henderson © 2003 National Geographic Society, photos (top) © Bill Hatcher/NGIC, (bottom) © Steve McCurry; page 35-c © Wolfgang Kaehler/Corbis; page 35-d © Peter Turnley/Corbis; page 36 © Angelo Hornak/Corbis.

Produced through the worldwide resources of the National Geographic Society, John M. Fahey, Jr., President and Chief Executive Officer; Gilbert M. Grosvenor, Chairman of the Board; Nina D. Hoffman, Executive Vice President and President, Books and Education Publishing Group.

PREPARED BY NATIONAL GEOGRAPHIC SCHOOL PUBLISHING
Ericka Markman, Senior Vice President and President, Children's Books and Education Publishing Group; Steve Mico, Senior Vice President, Editorial Director, Publisher; Francis Downey, Executive Editor; Richard Easby, Editorial Manager; Anne Stone, Lori Dibble Collins, Editors; Jim Hiscott, Design Manager; Cynthia Olson, Art Director; Margaret Sidlosky, Illustrations Director; Matt Wascavage, Manager of Publishing Services; Sean Philpotts, Jane Ponton, Production Managers; Ted Tucker, Production Specialist.

MANUFACTURING AND QUALITY CONTROL
Christopher A. Liedel, Chief Financial Officer; Phillip L. Schlosser, Director; Clifton M. Brown III, Manager.

◀ Newly dyed clothes are hung to dry at a factory in India.

Contents

CONSULTANT AND REVIEWER
Dr. V.V. Raman, Ph.D., Emeritus Professor, Rochester Institute of
Technology, Rochester, New York

BOOK DESIGN/PHOTO RESEARCH
Steve Curtis Design, Inc.

Published by the National Geographic Society
1145 17th Street N.W.
Washington, D.C. 20036-4688

ISBN-13: 978-0-7922-5466-9
ISBN-10: 0-7922-5466-X

2014
    3 4 5 6 7 8 9 10 11 12 13 14 15

Printed in Canada.

India Today

India is a big country in southern Asia. India has tall mountains. It also has rain forests and deserts. Most people in India live in small towns or villages. But India also has huge cities. More than one billion people live in India. Only China has more people than India has.

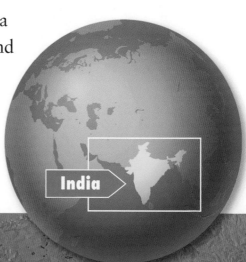

▲ The Himalaya Mountains

▲ The Great Indian Desert, sometimes called the Thar Desert

▲ The Darjiling Forest

▲ The city of Mumbai, sometimes called Bombay

Big Idea
Ancient India was home to one of the earliest great civilizations.

Set Purpose
Learn about life in ancient India.

India's

India has a long and rich history. People have lived here for thousands of years. India was home to one of the world's first great **civilizations.** Scientists came up with many important ideas. People created new religions. They built great cities and temples. What remains today from **ancient** times?

civilization – a highly developed culture

ancient – very old or from very long ago

Questions You Will Explore

What was life like in ancient India?

What ideas from ancient India are still around today?

Rich History

▲ This is Varanasi, one of the oldest cities in India.

Hinduism

Four world religions started in India. Three of these are from ancient times. They are Hinduism, Buddhism, and Jainism. The fourth religion is Sikhism. It started much later.

In **Hinduism,** there is one god. This god has many forms and many names. Hinduism teaches people that doing bad things will hurt them. Hinduism also divides people into groups, or **castes.** These castes are based on people's jobs. Each caste is a different social class. Today, most Indians are Hindu.

▲ This is one form of the Hindu god.

Hinduism – one of the oldest religions in India

caste – a Hindu social class

▼ Sometimes the Hindu god looks like this instead.

Buddhism

Buddhism is another religion that started in ancient India. Buddhism does not have gods. Buddhists follow the teachings of a man born long ago. That man is called Buddha.

Buddha wanted people to find happiness. So he taught them new ways to think and act. He thought this would help people live better. Not many Buddhists are left in India today. Yet the religion has spread around the world.

Buddhism – a religion based on the ideas of a great Indian teacher

▼ These are Buddhist monks in India.

Food

Religion changed the way people ate. In Hinduism, cows were sacred animals. So Hindus never ate beef. In Jainism, people were taught not to hurt others. So Jainists ate no meat. Instead, they ate bread, rice, and grains. They ate fruits and vegetables, too. Today, many Indians follow these same religions. They also eat many of the same foods.

▼ Indian food uses many fruits, vegetables, and grains.

Clothing

Ancient India was hot. People wore loose clothes to keep cool. Men wore **dhotis.** A dhoti is a long piece of cloth. Men wrapped it around their legs and tied it at the waist. Women wore **saris.** A sari is a piece of cloth that is worn like a dress. Some people also wore earrings and armbands. Some wore rings on their fingers and toes. Many people still dress in these traditional ways.

dhoti – a piece of clothing that is wrapped around the legs and tied at the waist

sari – a piece of cloth that is wrapped around the shoulders and waist and worn as a dress

▼ **Loose clothing is still popular in India today.**

Trade

People came from far away to trade for Indian goods. Traders came from Greece and Egypt. They traveled from China, too. Many traders wanted spices. Others wanted rice. People also wanted jewelry or cotton cloth. India is still known for these goods today.

Indian Trade Goods

Spices

Rice

Jewelry

Cotton cloth

Working Life

Many people lived and worked in cities. Builders made temples of stone. Some of their temples are still standing today. Other people owned shops. Still others worked at crafts. They made jewelry or wove cloth. Blacksmiths made metal tools. But most people were farmers. They raised food to eat and sell.

▼ Some ancient temples, such as this one, are still standing today.

Ancient Art

India's **golden age** lasted from 320–500.
During those years, the country was at peace.
People had time for things such as art.
Painters decorated the walls of temples.
Writers wrote poetry and plays. Artists made
sculptures of copper. People also made gold
and silver coins. These coins had beautiful
designs. Today, people study the coins and
art to learn about ancient times.

....

golden age – a time of great cultural success

◀ **These are gold coins
from ancient India.**

▼ **Ancient India was known for
its art. Here, a craftsman
works with gold.**

Gifts for the Future

Ancient India was also home to many doctors and scientists. Scientists studied the planets and stars. Doctors knew how to treat broken bones. They found cures for many illnesses. They even learned to operate. The people of ancient India created a great civilization. Many of their ideas are still around today.

Stop and Think!

What traditions from ancient India are still around today?

▼ Scientists in later times learned from ancient Indian discoveries.

15

Life Along the

Recap
Explain what traditions survive from ancient India.

Set Purpose
Learn what life is like in northern India today.

▲ The Ganga River winds through northern India.

Ganga

The Ganga, or Ganges, is a river. It starts high in the mountains. Then it flows through northern India. Finally, it empties into the Indian Ocean. The Ganga is the longest river in India.

Many people depend on the river. Hindus believe the Ganga is holy. Farmers use the Ganga to water their crops. People travel along the river in boats. The Ganga brings life to India.

The Beginning of the Ganga

The Himalaya are mountains. They are the highest mountains in the world. Some of the Himalaya are in India. The mountains are covered with ice and snow. In spring, the snow melts. It runs down the mountains. In summer, rains run down. This water forms the Ganga River.

▲ Snow from the mountains helps form the Ganga River.

Down From the Mountains

At first, water rushes down from the mountains. It moves so fast that it carries mud and tiny bits of rock with it. In time, the river reaches flatter ground. It gets wider. The water moves slower. It can no longer carry the mud. So the river drops the mud on the soil nearby. The mud makes very good farmland.

▼ The river slows when it reaches flatter ground.

Farms Along the Ganga

In ancient times, many farmers lived near the Ganga. Today, they still do. The soil near the river is good for farming. The river helps farmers water their crops. Most farms are small. Yet farmers grow a lot of food. Their crops feed 300 million people.

▲ A farmer works in a field near the Ganga River.

Family Life

Families are important in India. Many people come from large families. Sometimes parents, children, and grandparents live together. They work on farms, like people did long ago. Other times, children move to the city. They can earn more money there. Often, they send money back home to their families.

▼ A farming family takes a break together.

The Holy City of Varanasi

There are many cities along the Ganga. One city is Varanasi, or Banaras. This is one of the oldest cities in the world. Varanasi is a holy city. Millions of Hindus visit Varanasi each year. People come to pray. They also come to bathe in the river. Hindus believe the Ganga will wash away bad things that they have done.

▼ Hindus bathe in the Ganga.

The City of Kolkata

Near its end, the Ganga splits into many smaller rivers. The city of Kolkata, or Calcutta, is on one of these rivers. Kolkata has a huge **port.** Ships come to pick up and drop off goods.

Kolkata is the largest city in India. More than 14 million people live here, near the river's end. The city is known for its art, science, and poetry. It carries on traditions of long ago.

....

port – a harbor where ships load and unload goods

Stop and Think!

What is life like along the Ganga today?

▼ Kolkata is crowded with people and cars.

Recap
Tell about life along the Ganga River today.

Set Purpose
Learn more about life in India.

CONNECT WHAT YOU HAVE LEARNED

India in the Past and Present

Ancient India was home to a great civilization. Many ideas and traditions remain today from ancient India.

Here are some ideas that you learned about India.

- Hinduism and Buddhism both started in ancient India.
- Ancient India had great artists, doctors, and scientists.
- Many people in India today are farmers, just as in ancient times.
- India has many crowded cities today.

Check What You Have Learned

What made ancient India a great civilization?

▲ Many Indian temples were built in ancient times.

▲ Scientists in later times learned from ancient Indian discoveries.

▲ Farmers depend on the Ganga for water and healthy crops.

▲ Today, many people in India live in big cities.

▲ Getting around can be hard during the monsoon season.

Monsoons

Monsoons are very strong winds. Summer monsoons blow from the ocean toward land. The winds bring huge rainstorms. The rain often ruins homes and farms. But the monsoons help the Indian people, too. Monsoons cool the summer heat. They provide water for drinking and cooking. They give farmers water to grow their crops.

The Taj Mahal

India had a ruler named Shah Jahan. He had many wives. His favorite was named Mumtaz. When she died, Shah Jahan was heartbroken. He decided to make a beautiful tomb for Mumtaz. Twenty thousand workers helped build the tomb. One thousand elephants also helped. The tomb took more than ten years to build. Today, the Taj Mahal is one of the most famous buildings in India.

▼ **The Taj Mahal is a very famous building in India.**

▲ An elephant carries a
large load of branches.

Elephants

Indian elephants are hard workers. They help
people do many things. Elephants can carry
heavy loads. They were once used to help
fight wars. Soldiers rode them into battle.

Taking care of an elephant is hard. Elephants
eat for 20 hours each day. Every day, they eat
up to 600 pounds of grass and leaves!

Pajamas

Do you wear pajamas to bed? Do you know how this tradition started? The British saw people in India wearing loose pants. The pants looked very comfortable. The British decided to wear them, too. Indians wore pajamas in the daytime. But the British only wore them for bed.

▼ **Loose pajamas are cool in the heat of summer.**

Many kinds of words are used in this book. Here you will learn about words that show action. You will also learn about words that have a suffix.

Verbs

A verb is a word that shows action. Find the verbs below. Use each word in a sentence of your own.

Craftsmen **worked** with gold.

Scientists **studied** the stars.

Water **rushes** down from the mountains.

Hindus **bathe** in the Ganga.

Suffixes

A suffix is a group of letters added to the end of a word. A suffix changes the meaning of the word. For example, the suffix *-er* means "more." The suffix *-est* means "most."

Most farms in India are **smaller** than farms in America.

The river slows when it reaches **flatter** ground.

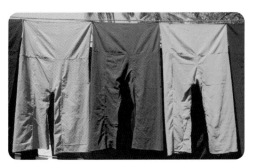

Pajamas are **looser** than many other kinds of pants.

The Ganga is the **longest** river in India.

Varanasi is one of India's **oldest** cities.

Kolkata is the **largest** city in the country.

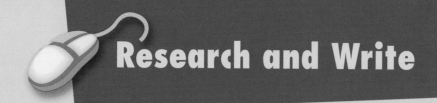

Research and Write

Write About Ancient India

You read about life in ancient India. Now learn more about the golden age. What did people discover about science? What did they learn about math? What did they know about art?

Research

Collect books and reference materials, or go online.

Read and Take Notes

As you read, take notes and draw pictures.

Write

Write about a discovery from ancient India. Describe the discovery. Tell who made the discovery. Explain why it was important.

▶ **An ancient Indian temple**

Read and Compare

Read More About India

Find and read other books about India. As you read, think about these questions.

- What is life like in India today?
- What role does India's history play in life today?
- Why is India important in the world today?

Books to Read

▲ Learn more about India in the past and present.

▲ Discover other ancient civilizations of West Asia.

▲ Explore India's land and climate.

Glossary

KEY CONCEPT

ancient (page 6)
Very old or from very long ago
Some ancient temples are still standing today.

KEY CONCEPT

Buddhism (page 9)
A religion based on the ideas of a great Indian teacher
Buddhism started in ancient India.

KEY CONCEPT

caste (page 8)
A Hindu social class
People with certain jobs, such as priests, were in the highest caste.

KEY CONCEPT

civilization (page 6)
A highly developed culture
Ancient India was a great civilization.

dhoti (page 11)
A piece of clothing that is wrapped around the legs and tied at the waist
Many men in India still like to wear a dhoti.

golden age (page 14)
A time of great cultural success
India made beautiful art during its golden age.

Hinduism (page 8)
One of the oldest religions in India
Hinduism has a god known by many different names.

port (page 23)
A harbor where ships load and unload goods
Kolkata has a large and busy port.

sari (page 11)
A piece of cloth that is wrapped around the shoulders
and waist and worn as a dress
Today, an Indian woman might still dress in a sari.

Index